SECOND CHRONICLES
seven:
fourteen

A 28-DAY JOURNEY IN PRAYER

JAMES T. BRADFORD

Published by My Healthy Church
1445 N. Boonville Ave., Springfield, Missouri 65802.

Cover design by Prodigy Pixel of Springfield, Missouri.

ISBN: 978-1-62423-040-0

First printing 2013
Printed in the United States of America.

Contents

THE 7:14 CALL TO PRAYER

God's prescription for renewal has not changed. He assured Israel in 2 Chronicles 7:14:

> "If my people who are called by my name, will humble themselves and pray and seek my face and turn from their wicked ways, then will I hear from heaven and will forgive their sin and heal their land."

Today, the Spirit of God calls Christ's living church to humility, hunger for God, and holiness. This call has always been at the heart of God when He is preparing to do a new work.

We are hearing this call afresh—a 7:14 Call to Prayer. The urgency behind this initiative is born of a prophetic sense that God is preparing our churches and our nation for renewal and spiritual awakening.

This is how you can participate in this call to prayer:

- Every day, take a moment at 7:14 a.m. and 7:14 p.m. to pray for spiritual awakening in all of its dimensions. The 7:14 Prayer app is now available to assist with these daily moments of prayer.

- Every week, join the leadership of our Fellowship and commit to fast and pray over the noon hour on Friday (or another day in the week that works for you).

- For four weeks, use this prayer book as a daily guide on a journey of prayer for your life, your family, your church community, our nation, and the world. The prayer journey begins with you and your worship of God and gradually extends outward to prayer for the unreached.

Before you begin Day 1 of the 7:14 Call to Prayer, take a few minutes to read the introduction on The Priority of Prayer and the short guide on How to Pray. I offer these simply as a way to remind ourselves why we pray and to encourage you with a simple outline for prayer as you step into the 7:14 Call to Prayer.

Included among the daily guided prayers are thoughts on kinds of prayers to pray, Bible verses on prayer, and other small resources to help develop your prayer life.

So here we are. Let us seek God together for one more Jesus-centered spiritual awakening in America.

Introduction

THE PRIORITY OF PRAYER: WHAT WILL IT COST?

At the Lausanne Conference in 2010, a Pentecostal Kenyan preacher told a story of the revival in East Africa fifty years ago. The people walked well-worn paths to prayer huts in the bush. As the revival progressed, if people stopped going to the place of prayer, they would gently encourage each other: "I see that grass is growing on your path." When it comes to finding and establishing the place of prayer in our lives, may grass not grow on our paths.

The apostle Paul talks about our problem in prayer in Ephesians 6:

> For our struggle is not against flesh and blood, but against the rulers, against the authorities, against the powers of this dark world and against the spiritual forces of evil in the heavenly realms. (Ephesians 6:12)

Our battle is not the economy in our country or the critic who comes to ruin our day. Our battle is not with people. Paul says that our struggle is against rulers, authorities, powers of this dark world, and spiritual forces of evil. The priority of prayer can easily become rhetoric to us. We say, "I know I ought to pray but . . ." As a result, we are known for our external activity rather than our internal life of prayer. By putting the emphasis on the external, we live in denial of what Paul clearly says is the center of our battle. Prayer shifts our focus to where the battle truly happens—in the heavenly places.

Samuel Chadwick said, "The one concern of the devil is to keep Christians from praying. He fears nothing from prayerless studies, prayerless work, and prayerless religion. He laughs at our toil, mocks at our wisdom, but trembles when we pray." The priority of prayer reaffirms the center of the true spiritual battle—it is in the spiritual realms with the realities of powers, authorities, and forces of evil.

I encourage you, at a time when God is calling people across this nation to pray, to ask yourself the question: What will it cost me?

For most of us, a deepened life in prayer will cost us something tangible: time, a possession, or an activity or hobby. Time spent in prayer refocuses our daily priorities; it is no longer about us, but it is about God. Our goals are reshaped in order to better please Him and live a life more dependent on the leading of the Holy Spirit. So ask yourself the question honestly, even as I ask myself the same question, and let us be willing to die to ourselves and be people of faith in heightened ways.

A PATTERN FOR PRAYER

When we rely on organization, we get what organization can do.
When we rely on education, we get what education can do.
When we rely on eloquence, we get what eloquence can do.
When we rely on prayer, we get what God can do.
—A. C. Dixon

Nehemiah 1 offers us a pattern for prayer, and we can use the word PRAY to follow this pattern. I encourage you to use this simple device as you enter into the 7:14 prayer initiative.

Praise
Then I said: "Lord, the God of heaven, the great and awesome God, who keeps his covenant of love with those who love him and keep his commandments." (Nehemiah 1:5)

In praise, Nehemiah identified those attributes of God that he needed to call upon if he was going to rebuild the walls of Jerusalem, for the provisions he needed, and for the favor of God.

He said, "God, you are a God who keeps covenant. This is your covenant city and these are your covenant people. You are great and awesome." This is the kind of God Nehemiah needed because the task was impossible. Great praying starts with praise, not with the need; it focuses first on the capacity of God to address the problem.

Repent
"Lord . . . let your ear be attentive and your eyes open to hear the prayer

9

your servant is praying before you day and night for your servants, the people of Israel. I confess the sins we Israelites, including myself and my father's family, have committed against you. We have acted very wickedly toward you. We have not obeyed the commands, decrees and laws you gave your servant Moses." (Nehemiah 1:5–7)

The next thing Nehemiah did was to repent. He repented for all those things that had contributed to this brokenness. He repented for himself, and he repented on behalf of the whole nation. Repentance is the door opener to God's kingdom and rule. Repentance is saying, "God, my way is wrong, and I turn from my way."

Ask

"Remember the instruction you gave your servant Moses, saying, 'If you are unfaithful, I will scatter you among the nations, but if you return to me and obey my commands, then even if your exiled people are at the farthest horizon, I will gather them from there and bring them to the place I have chosen as a dwelling for my Name.' They are your servants and your people, whom you redeemed by your great strength and your mighty hand. Lord, let your ear be attentive to the prayer of this your servant and to the prayer of your servants who delight in revering your name." (Nehemiah 1:8–11)

Nehemiah asked for the favor and capacity to rebuild the walls by reminding God of His promises. He spoke directly to God's heart: "Lord, these are your servants and the people you redeemed by your strength, so let your ear be attentive to our prayer."

He shaped the whole request of what he needed from God by quoting promises to God. There are promises from God's Word that I keep close and quote out loud when I pray. I say, "This is what you promised, Lord, and I trust you for these things."

Yield

"Give your servant success today by granting him favor in the presence of this man." (Nehemiah 1:11)

At the end of his prayer, Nehemiah yielded to God. He said, "Give your servant success today by granting him favor in the presence of this man, the king." In other words, "Lord, if I can be a part of the answer to this prayer, I yield myself to you." What a wonderful way to end prayer.

Years ago, when we taught our daughters how to pray using this pattern, "yield" was a big word for children, so they substituted the word "yes." That's really what yielding is. It's saying yes to God's will, yes to the coming of His Spirit, yes to whatever He has for me today.

Second Chronicles Seven: Fourteen

Introduction

Hurricane Sandy was headed for the East Coast at the same time I was, so I canceled my trip to Boston at the last minute. This change in plans allowed me to attend my home church in Springfield, Missouri, where Central Bible College president Dr. Gary Denbow preached on the topic of prayer. Since I was preparing for this book, I thought, What timing! His message entitled "Prepare to Pray" felt like the right place for us to start our four-week prayer journey, so with Dr. Denbow's permission, I share these thoughts with you.

Drawing from Daniel 10, we see Daniel is the perfect example of a prayer warrior. What Daniel experienced in his prayer times offers us insight as to what we might also experience when we enter the ministry of prayer.

1. Prepare to pray effectively.

At that time I, Daniel, mourned for three weeks. I ate no choice food; no meat or wine touched my lips; and I used no lotions at all until the three weeks were over. (Daniel 10:2, 3)

Prayer should be viewed as foundational to the ministry that God has called us to fulfill. We should be diligent in planning our prayer time. We should be willing to give up or lay aside anything that would deter us from praying.

2. Prepare to pray alone.

I, Daniel, was the only one who saw the vision; those who were with me did not see it, but such terror overwhelmed them that they fled and hid themselves. (Daniel 10:7)

Prayer is hard work. Prayer is not a restricted calling. It is a foundational spiritual discipline for every believer. Don't shun the supernatural!

3. Prepare to expend a lot of energy when you pray.

So I was left alone, gazing at this great vision; I had no strength left, my face turned deathly pale and I was helpless . . . "How can I, your servant, talk with you, my lord? My strength is gone and I can hardly breathe." (Daniel 10:8, 17)

An emptying may be needed before a filling can take place. Depleting all human resources is sometimes necessary before you and I can fully depend on the Lord.

4. Prepare to be attacked when you pray.

But the prince of the Persian kingdom resisted me twenty-one days. Then Michael, one of the chief princes, came to help me, because I was detained there with the king of Persia. (Daniel 10:13)

The enemy of our souls uses every imaginable way to divert us from praying. The enemy fights against the accomplishment of God's will.

5. Prepare to be ushered into the supernatural when you pray.

I looked up and there before me was a man dressed in linen, with a belt of fine gold from Uphaz around his waist. . . . A hand touched me and set me trembling on my hands and knees. . . . Again the one who looked like a man touched me and gave me strength. (Daniel 10:5, 10, 18)

Can we, by faith, raise our expectations to a point that we are not taken aback when our Lord appears? It is possible—and likely—that signs, wonders, and miracles will happen when we pray.

6. Prepare to be changed when you pray.

He said, "Daniel, you who are highly esteemed, consider carefully the words I am about to speak to you, and stand up, for I have now been sent to you." And when he said this to me, I stood up trembling. . . . "Now I have come to explain to you what will happen to your people in the future, for the vision concerns a time yet to come. . . ." Then one who looked like a man touched my lips, and I opened my mouth and began to speak. I said to the one standing before me, "I am overcome with anguish because of the vision, my lord, and I feel very weak." (Daniel 10:11, 14, 16)

Before moving forward, declare three things regarding the ministry of prayer:

1. I will make a new commitment to take whatever steps necessary to make prayer a priority in my daily life.

2. I will commit to being a part of the ministry of prayer of this church, praying for the needs of this community, this state, my country, and the peoples of the earth.

3. I will be filled with the Spirit of God and be ready for whatever He gives.

Ready for Week 1?

This four-week prayer journey begins with God. During Week 1, each of us will worship and respond to God as those created in His image and for His glory. Over the course of the next seven days we will worship God and allow Him to prepare us from the inside out to pray according to His will for our families, our churches, our nation, and the world.

Day 1
Worship God

Stand in God's Supremacy

Our God is in heaven; He does whatever pleases him. (Psalm 115:3)

We can be confident in prayer because God is supreme. Because He is supreme, then no problem that we pray about can out-muscle our God. No spiritual power that comes against us can defeat Him. His supremacy means that He is sovereign and strong, ruling over all, and more powerful than anything.

I look at Psalm 115:3 as the ultimate statement on God's supremacy. In the previous verse the neighboring idol-worshiping nations asked Israel, "Where is your God?" They were saying, "We can see our wood and stone gods sitting on the shelves in our homes. But we can't see Israel's God." The answer? "Our God is in heaven; He does whatever pleases Him." God is in heaven, so you can't contain Him; and He does whatever He wants, so you can't control Him.

This is the God we seek in prayer today—alive, loose, and unconstrained. And when we pray according to His sovereign will, His supremacy steps into our defeated, captive situations to restore and free us.

Pray the Scriptures:

Psalm 8
Psalm 135
Romans 11:33–36

Focus Today:

Declare the supremacy of God in your life today. Answer God as Job did, "I know that you can do all things, and that no purpose of yours can be thwarted." Stand confident in God and believe that His plan will be done.

_____

_____

_____

_____

_____

_____

_____

_____

_____

_____

_____

_____

_____

_____

_____

_____

_____

_____

When I consider your heavens, the work of your fingers,
the moon and stars, which you have set in place,
what is mankind that you are mindful of them. (Psalm 8:3)

Day 2
Worship God

Consider God's Authority

A powerful storm produces wall-shaking, window-rattling thunder—the kind that for a split second makes you think that Jesus is near. The people of Israel encountered such thunder when God descended on Mt. Sinai with smoke and fire. The people trembled, Moses spoke, and "God answered him in thunder" (Exodus 19:19).

But sometimes in the storms, thunder is heard as a soft rumble in the distance. Sometimes a quieter voice reveals God's authority and power. Elijah was hiding in a cave when God passed by. There was wind, an earthquake, and fire, but God was not in any of them. Elijah approached the opening of the cave with his face covered and heard the voice of God. God was not in the loud, spectacular moments but in a simple voice.

What is God doing in your life right now? Is He shaking your world and trying to get your attention, or is He asking you to listen for Him and respond in full submission? How will you encounter the authority of God today—in the booming thunder or in the still small voice?

Pray the Scriptures:

1 Kings 19:9–13
Job 37:1–7
Revelation 12:10–12

Focus Today:

Consider today's weather and God's control over it. Praise Him for His authority over the earth and weather patterns. Take time today to worship God and put yourself under His protective authority.

_____

_____

_____

_____

_____

_____

_____

_____

_____

_____

_____

_____

_____

_____

_____

_____

_____

_____

_____

He says to the snow, "Fall on the earth," and to the rain shower,
"Be a mighty downpour." (Job 37:5)

Day 3
Worship God

Embrace God's Capacity

As a pastor I often heard people say, "I feel guilty when I pray for my own needs. After all, God has so many people to take care of." In essence they are saying, "If God meets my needs, it will deplete Him in such a way that He cannot meet the needs of others."

> Do you not know? Have you not heard? The LORD is the everlasting God, the Creator of the ends of the earth. He will not grow tired or weary, and his understanding no one can fathom. (Isaiah 40:28)

This verse asserts that as Creator, God's capacity can never be depleted. He is limitless and infinite. In mathematics, when you divide the number "infinity" by two, you get infinity. Infinity is the same thing as limitlessness, and you cannot divide limitlessness into anything smaller. Even if you divide infinity by seven billion, the population of the earth, you still get infinity. In other words, God's grace is infinitely and always available to each one of us.

Nothing is impossible for Him. Neither does His love for us have any limits. Prayer is more than twisting the arm of a reluctant God; it is embracing the heart of a loving, willing God. It is said of Jesus that as He went to heal the sick He was "moved with compassion." As we pray, we, too, can experience a dimension of His limitless love for others, and even for ourselves. This is "faith working through love" according to the apostle Paul in Galatians 5:6. Embrace God and His vast capacity today; know and share His limitless love.

Pray the Scriptures:
Isaiah 40:28–31
Jeremiah 31:3–6
Matthew 9:35–38
Ephesians 3:14–21

Focus Today:

Thank God for His limitless capacity to love, forgive, and heal. Take time to dwell on the immensity of His love and ask God to increase the capacity of your heart to love.

_____

_____

_____

_____

_____

_____

_____

_____

_____

_____

_____

_____

_____

_____

_____

_____

_____

When he saw the crowds, he had compassion on them, because they were harassed and helpless, like sheep without a shepherd. (Matthew 9:36)

Day 4
Open Your Heart

Pursue Integrity

In mathematics an integer is a whole number and not a fraction. Integrity is exactly like that; it cannot be fractionalized. There is no room for secret patterns of questionable behaviors that are out of sync with our public image. People tend to rationalize and compartmentalize, but any patterns of secrecy should set off alarm bells inside and shake us into ruthless, internal honesty.

It's more than a cliché to say that our secrets keep us sick. Yet into the very center of the dark, secret places God planted the cross and hung His Son on it. This is our hope—God meets us at our worst, calls us to the painful honesty of confession, forgivingly frees us, and then recreates us with His resurrection Spirit. Integrity is possible because of this.

Pray the Scriptures:

1 Kings 9:4, 5
Psalm 41:11–13
Proverbs 2:6–8
Titus 2:7, 8

Focus Today:

Ask yourself, "Are there areas of ongoing secrecy in my life that I am intentionally hiding from those closest to me?" Open your heart to God and ask Him to reveal those areas to you.

_____

_____

_____

_____

_____

_____

_____

_____

_____

_____

_____

_____

_____

_____

_____

_____

_____

_____

_____

_____

_____

_____

In everything set them an example by doing what is good. (Titus 2:7)

Day 5
Mind

Fight for the Mind

Our minds are wonderful gifts from God. They are the means by which we process the world around us, make choices, navigate our way through life, and bring immense creativity and color to the human experience. It is also with our minds that we perceive God's truth and, based upon that truth, we are transformed by the renewing of our minds.

It should be no surprise, then, that our minds are also strategic targets for Satan, a spiritual battleground if you will. When the enemy has his way, our minds harbor debilitating doubts, embrace crippling lies, entertain false affections, and rationalize sin.

This battle with our minds becomes especially strong when we make the decision to pray. We find ourselves saying things like "I'm too tired. I'm unworthy. This is useless; God would never listen to someone like me. God doesn't care. I don't feel anything so I must not be spiritual enough."

And this is where we need to be relentless with the truth of who we are in Christ. We can win this battle with our minds. Through Jesus' triumph on the cross and by the power of His Spirit, we have all the spiritual weapons we need to "take captive every thought to make it obedient to Christ" (2 Corinthians 10:5).

Pray the Scriptures:

Romans 12:1, 2
2 Corinthians 10:3–5
Philippians 4:7–9
1 Peter 5:6–9

Focus Today:

Turn off the distracting voices in your head that would keep you from prayer. Instead, think about things that are true, noble, right, pure, lovely, and admirable and allow God to renew your mind.

_____

_____

_____

_____

_____

_____

_____

_____

_____

_____

_____

_____

_____

_____

*Do not conform to the pattern of this world, but be transformed
by the renewing of your mind. (Romans 12:1)*

Day 6
Body

Starve the Body

In a culture where the landscape is dotted with shrines to the Golden Arches and an assortment of Pizza Temples, fasting seems out of place, out of step with the times.

—Richard Foster, *Celebration of Discipline*

Fasting is not always a popular subject, but it is a subject that can open up a whole new world of spiritual growth for us.

Jesus answered, "It is written: 'Man shall not live on bread alone, but on every word that comes from the mouth of God.'" (Matthew 4:4)

Fasting redirects a hunger for bread to a hunger for God. It leaves space for a yearning for the presence of Jesus. He declared it inappropriate for His followers to fast while He was with them. But the day has come when we should yearn for His presence, and fasting redirects physical hunger into spiritual hunger, giving power to our prayers.

"For, as I have often told you before and now tell you again even with tears, many live as enemies of the cross of Christ. Their destiny is destruction, their god is their stomach, and their glory is in their shame. Their mind is set on earthly things." (Philippians 3:18, 19)

Fasting confronts the ungodly appetites in our lives. The stomach can be a principle source for those appetites, where eating becomes a way to fill up emotional potholes. When we fast and pray, we draw attention away from those potholes of lust and greed, comfort and security, happiness and pleasure of this earth, and we draw our attention to God.

While they were worshiping the Lord and fasting, the Holy Spirit said, "Set apart for me Barnabas and Saul for the work to which I have called them." So after they had fasted and prayed, they placed their hands on them and sent them off. (Acts 13:2, 3)

Fasting sharpens our discernment and releases God's power. It affixes us to spiritual realities and gives us sensitivity to the Holy Spirit. Fasting sharpens us to the direction and word of the Lord.

Pray the Scriptures:

Daniel 9:3–19
Joel 2:12, 13
2 Corinthians 12:9, 10

Focus Today:

Fast something today, be it food, coffee, or entertainment, and give the time you would spend enjoying those things to prayer and God's Word. Don't be surprised if God confronts you about other unhealthy appetites in your life.

_____

_____

_____

_____

_____

_____

_____

_____

But he said to me, "My grace is sufficient for you, for my power is made perfect in weakness." Therefore I will boast all the more gladly about my weaknesses, so that Christ's power may rest on me." (2 Corinthians 12:9)

Day 7
Vision
See with Spiritual Eyes

He [Abraham] is our father in the sight of God, in whom he believed—the God who gives life to the dead and calls things that are not as though they were. (Romans 4:17)

There are two kinds of sight—physical and spiritual. We see and react to what is in front of us using physical sight. Spiritual sight does not see what is in front of us, but it sees what is possible by faith. Abraham, often called the "Father of Faith," had this kind of spiritual vision; he could trust a God who remarkably "calls things that are not as though they were."

The spiritual eyesight that comes with faith makes the unseen so real that we begin to live as if it were real. Abraham did this. In Romans 4 we read that he trusted in a God who could call things that are not as though they were.

Against all hope, Abraham in hope believed. . . . Without weakening in his faith, he faced the fact that his body was as good as dead—since he was about a hundred years old—and that Sarah's womb was also dead. Yet he did not waver through unbelief regarding the promise of God, but was strengthened in his faith and gave glory to God. (Romans 4:18–20)

This is spiritual sight over physical sight: the certainty of God's promise over the seeming certainty of what we see. Take hold of the words of Paul in 2 Corinthians 5:7, "We live by faith, not by sight," and as you pray the scriptures today, consider the stories of people who believed a word from God that appeared impossible.

Pray the Scriptures:

Genesis 15:1–6
Luke 1:26–38
Luke 1:5–25, 57–66

Focus Today:

Has God spoken promises to you that seem too big to happen? Ask Him for the faith to see them through fresh spiritual eyes. Praise Him for His faithfulness to bring those promises to completion.

_____

_____

_____

_____

_____

_____

_____

_____

_____

_____

_____

_____

_____

_____

He took him outside and said, "Look up at the sky and count the stars—
if indeed you can count them." Then he said to him,
"So shall your offspring be." (Genesis 15:5)

Week 1 Reflection
Breakthrough Prayer

Our church forefathers used the phrase "pray through." We don't hear that phrase much anymore. The phrase describes breakthrough praying. It is a different kind of praying, something more than praying through a list of requests.

In the book of Nehemiah, Jerusalem's walls were broken and the gates were burned. The walls of a city kept it safe from the enemy, and business transactions happened at the gates. Without walls a city was vulnerable, and without gates there was a loss of function in the city. God used Nehemiah to repair the walls and gates, thereby bringing protection from the enemy and function back to the city.

But we read in Nehemiah 1, before he raised the resources and spoke to leaders for the task, he allowed the broken walls and burned gates to break his heart. It says in Nehemiah 1:4 that he sat down and wept. The image of Jerusalem vulnerable to its enemies and devoid of its God-given function ruined his heart. He then devoted himself to deep passionate prayer "for some days." Not just an hour, but for some days he mourned, fasted, and prayed.

This is called "breakthrough praying" because it lasts longer than one minute on one request. It is prolonged agony of spirit. In Romans 8, Paul says that sometimes we do not know how to pray but the Spirit prays through us with groanings that cannot be uttered. Our forefathers called it "travailing in the Spirit." It is those times that our hearts are gripped by the heart of God. It is more than a prayer request; it is a prayer agony.

This kind of prayer brings breakthrough and new birth. God wants to birth whole new seasons of life in our nation, in our churches, families, and in our lives, and sometimes the only place to start is by travail that leads to new birth.

Week 1 Reflection

_____

_____

_____

_____

_____

_____

_____

_____

_____

_____

_____

_____

_____

_____

_____

_____

_____

_____

_____

Week 2

Introduction

One day, before my wife and I were engaged, we were driving down the freeway, and she asked me, "Why don't we ever pray together?"

At the time I was a single pastor of a growing congregation, and I answered, "You know, I pray with people all the time. It's my job." In other words, I told her, "You're not my job." As the words came out of my mouth, I thought, *I can't believe I just said that.* Those words were directly opposite to everything I believed about the fellowship of the Holy Spirit and what it meant to walk in the Spirit. Prayer is not something we relegate to certain kinds of relationships or vocations. Prayer is central to walking in the Holy Spirit and should permeate every relationship we have.

That moment (my saying a very stupid thing) changed our relationship. From that point forward, we committed to pray with each other, and at the end of each date we prayed together for fifteen to twenty minutes.

Once we were married, we made certain this habit was part of our weekly routine. When our two daughters were little, we waited until after they were in bed, around nine in the evening. We have found that spending this extended time in prayer together is extremely powerful.

Our typical prayer time looks like this: we spend the first thirty minutes asking each other how we can pray for the other. We found as a married couple that even though we could guess what each other would say, it was still good practice to ask and hear each other's responses. The context of these prayer requests often leads us into our deepest conversations of the week about what is happening in our hearts and relationship.

Then we spend one hour praying: praying for each other, our children, our extended families, and our close friends. Then we pray for those "mountain moving" needs in the church. We find real power in agreeing on all these things as husband and wife.

Ready for Week 2?

During Week 2, we move our prayer journey outward, starting with our families. It will look something like the weekly prayer times that my wife and I have—praying for spouses, children, extended family, and close friends—over the course of the next seven days. Take time this week to pray for specific needs of your family members.

Week 2 Introduction

Day 1
Spouse

Pray for Your Spouse

For those who are married, building spiritual intimacy with your husband or wife is important. There are three things you can implement to help build that intimacy:

1. Verbally express your prayer requests to each other, even if you think your spouse knows you well enough to know how to pray for you. This is humbling, but it helps cultivate openness and honesty in the relationship. This, in turn, opens you to the Holy Spirit's activity.

2. It is important to develop the confidence to pray conversationally—out loud—with others. The ideal place to start is with your own spouse, verbalizing prayers out loud as you pray together.

3. Praying for each other in spiritual agreement is powerful. I had been a full-time pastor for about fifteen years when I went through a season of discouragement that lasted for several months. There seemed no reason for it. The church was doing well, our family was doing well, and nothing bad was happening. I was just discouraged all the time, like I was living under an annoying cloud. One evening in our weekly prayer time, Sandi prayed fervently in Jesus' name that this discouragement would break and that the spiritual oppression disburse. I had never honestly heard her pray so aggressively for me, but something broke in the spiritual realm and the cloud of discouragement vanished.

There is power in praying together, and a deeper spiritual intimacy will develop as you share openly in conversation. Opening up invites healthy critique and accountability with your spouse, and agreeing in prayer places you both before a compassionate God.

Pray the Scriptures:

Psalm 145:17–21
Matthew 18:19, 20
Ephesians 5:31–33

Focus Today:

Take intentional time today to share prayer requests and pray out loud with your spouse.

Not everyone on this prayer journey has a spouse. If that is you, share this day's entry with a friend or family member who is married, and say a specific prayer for that couple today.

_____

_____

_____

_____

_____

_____

_____

_____

_____

_____

Again, truly I tell you that if two of you on earth agree about anything they ask for, it will be done for them by my Father in heaven. (Matthew 18:18)

Day 2
Children

Pray Over Your Children

I heard a story about a family—a father and mother with three children. Dad worked and mom stayed at home. As all three children started their years in school, each morning before sending the kids to the
bus stop, mom (and dad on his days off) would pray over the kids: "Dear
heavenly Father, we thank You for this day. We thank You for the life
you've given us. Bless these kids as they go to school. Keep them safe.
May they bring glory to You in all that they say and do. In Jesus' name,
amen."

Every morning from kindergarten through twelfth grade, they stopped
at the front door and mom or dad prayed the same prayer before those
children left the house. Thirteen years of school, three kids. No matter if they were on time or running late, if they were catching the bus
or driving themselves to school, a parent prayed for those children.

From what I understand, the children were not perfect angels. They
got into trouble, like any trio of siblings. But they kept to the path
of Jesus. There were no rebellious teenage years, no wandering from
their faith in college. The one who told me the story believes those
prayers every morning actually worked, that Jesus kept them close to
Himself through the power of praying parents. As adults, two of the
children are in mission work and the third is a successful salesman.

Pray over your children, and let your children hear those prayers. The
prayer does not need to be fancy, just authentic. Make it consistent
and a part of your daily routine.

Pray the Scriptures:

Deuteronomy 11:18–21
Psalm 127:3–5
Proverbs 22:6

Focus Today:

Take the example of the family above and apply it to your situation. Try two minutes before your children leave the house; speak a prayer over them and make it heartfelt.

Maybe your children are grown and no longer live in your house. It's never too late to start praying from them daily. If you don't have children of your own, pray for children in a family that you know well.

_____

_____

_____

_____

_____

_____

_____

_____

_____

_____

_____

_____

*Teach them to your children, talking about them when you sit at home
and when you walk along the road, when you lie down
and when you get up. (Deuteronomy 11:19)*

Day 3
Parents

Pray for Your Parents

Dick Eastman describes prayer as "love on its knees." Praying for our parents is a way of valuing our heritage, appreciating the role parents have played in our lives, and "loving them on our knees."

For those with painful, damaged relationships with parents, the discipline of regularly praying for them may require you to walk the pathway of forgiveness. You will need to let go of past hurt and begin to see your parents as God sees them. Prayer, no matter who it's for, always brings God's perspective on people and past experiences.

For some of us separated by long miles from parents, praying for them can help us feel close to them and connected to what is happening in their lives.

No matter the age or stage of life that our parents are in, they still have hearts and need prayer. Some of our parents, like mine, have prayed all of our lives for us—often without much reciprocation on our part. They now need prayer for God's will and purpose to be worked out in their lives, just as much as we needed it in days past. This is our opportunity to "love them on our knees," honor their role as our parents, and bring them regularly to God's own throne.

"Honor your father and your mother, so that you may live long in the land the Lord your God is giving you" (Exodus 20:12). This is the first of the Ten Commandments with a promise attached to it. As we love, honor, and pray for our parents, we can trust God our heavenly Father will answer His promises to us.

Pray the Scriptures:

Exodus 20:12
Ephesians 6:1–4

Focus Today:

Maybe you have a photo of your parents that you can pull out. Keep it handy for the day and thank God for the good memories. Perhaps it is painful for you to think about your parents. Pray that God would show you your parents through His eyes today.

_____

_____

_____

_____

_____

_____

_____

_____

_____

_____

_____

_____

_____

_____

_____

_____

_____

*Honor your father and your mother, so that you may live long
in the land the Lord your God is giving you. (Exodus 20:12)*

Day 4
Siblings

Pray for Your Siblings

My wife, Sandi, shares a wonderful testimony of standing with her brother Doug in prayer for healing.

> The summer of 1977 found our family in one of our most challenging seasons. My twenty-six-year-old brother was diagnosed with a vascular tumor in his knee. We were referred to MD Anderson Cancer Center in Houston for surgery.
>
> The post-op diagnosis called for six weeks of intense radiation, which would leave his leg immobile. The three-day weekend gave us time to fast and pray before beginning the radiation regimen. We stood on Psalm 118: 8, 17, 21: "It is better to trust the LORD than to put confidence in men. . . . I shall not die, but live to tell of all his deeds. . . . O LORD, thank you so much for answering my prayer and saving me."
>
> When we went back, my brother told the doctors that he believed God was asking him to trust for his complete healing and reject any further treatment. Today he is a missionary in Ethiopia and still runs every day.

Sandi's family joined together and stood on God's Word for Doug's healing. They fasted, prayed, sought God, and came away believing that healing would come from God—and it did. We cannot overlook the role of Scripture and standing on God's promises when we pray for our family members. When a sibling is hurting, we stand next to them and we stand on God's Word, believing for the healing that is needed.

Pray the Scriptures:

Jeremiah 29:11–13
Philippians 4:19
Romans 8:31–39

Focus Today:

Do you have a sibling with a need? Take one of the scriptures above and pray it together. Stand on God's promise for the fulfillment of that need.

Maybe you have a friend who feels like a brother or sister. If there is a need in your friend's life, join together in prayer, believing God's promise to meet it.

_____

_____

_____

_____

_____

_____

_____

_____

_____

_____

_____

And my God will meet all your needs according to the riches
of his glory in Christ Jesus. (Philippians 4:19)

Day 5
The Next Generation of Children

Pray for Your Grandchildren, Nieces, and Nephews

The Scriptures say much about God passing His blessing from generation to generation. The Lord declares Himself to be our "dwelling place" throughout all generations (Psalm 90:1).

This begins by praying for the salvation of our grandchildren, nieces, and nephews. Sandi and I do not have grandchildren yet, but I distinctly remember years ago the two of us praying through the list of our nieces and nephews. The Holy Spirit especially gripped our hearts in a time of extended intercession for one of our nephews. We felt God's heart strongly. Sandi began to weep, and together we called out to God for him. It was a vulnerable time for him spiritually. In the years since wonderful things have unfolded in his life to God's glory, and he now serves Jesus wholeheartedly.

Our prayers then go beyond salvation to encompass every aspect of life for this next generation. Since the day our daughters were born, Sandi and I have prayed for spiritual protection over them, God's call on their lives, their future spouses, and the daily details of their lives. We can then pray the same way for our grandchildren. Children need a grandparent, and spiritual grandparents, praying over them in this way.

We place our grandchildren, nieces, and nephews in God's hands. Some of these prayers may take a long while to be answered, but standing in faith over many years is an extremely important way of covering and supporting our families spiritually.

Pray the Scriptures:
Psalm 8:2
Matthew 18:1–5

Focus Today:

If your grandchildren, nieces, or nephews are nearby, spend time with them today and include a prayer of blessing over them. If they are at a distance, contact them and let them know you are praying for them.

Any friends with children will appreciate prayers of protection that you pray for them today.

_____

_____

_____

_____

_____

_____

_____

_____

_____

_____

_____

_____

_____

_____

And he said: "Truly I tell you, unless you change and become like little children, you will never enter the kingdom of heaven." (Matthew 18:3)

Day 6
Extended Family

Pray for Your Extended Family

There are uncles, aunts, cousins, and grandparents who are a circle or two removed from the spiritual influences of our own lives. Maybe we don't see them except at a family reunion or a cousin's wedding or during the holidays, and I sometimes wonder if these people have anyone praying for them. My life has been so graced and redirected by people praying for me—but what about them? We may be the only ones praying for them!

In Genesis 18 Abraham plead with the Lord for Sodom, the city where his nephew Lot lived. God destroyed it and Gomorrah but remembered Abraham, and He "brought Lot out of the catastrophe that overthrew the cities where Lot had lived" (Genesis 19:29). Job had a regular custom to make an altar and pray for his family, thinking, "Perhaps my children have sinned and cursed God in their hearts" (Job 1:5). Like Abraham and Lot, we must carry our family members before the Lord and pray for their salvation, claiming their lives for God's purposes and not the enemy's purposes.

Pray the Scriptures:

Genesis 18:16–33; 19:1–29
Job 1:5
Lamentations 3:22–26

Focus Today:

Make a list of your extended family members and ask the Holy Spirit to guide you in how to pray for them. Ask the Spirit to show you ways to connect with them. Through this connection, you may become part of the answer to your prayers.

_Because of the L_ORD_'s great love we are not consumed, for his compassions never fail. They are new every morning; great is your faithfulness._
(Lamentations 3:22)

Day 7
Mentors and Closest Friends

Pray for Your Inner Circle

There are some people in our lives who are not relatives, but we feel a special spiritual connection with them and pray more often for them. Jesus also had levels of relationships: John, then the three (Peter, James, and John), the twelve disciples, the seventy, the "larger group of disciples," and finally the multitudes.

These relationships nourish and resource us in life-giving ways. They are the people who serve as spiritual advisors and encouragers, personal friends and confidants. They are people who are gifts from God and whose friendship and influence in our lives we cherish.

I am amazed at how many times Paul begins his letters in the New Testament with statements like "I thank my God through Jesus Christ for all of you" (Romans 1:8), or even to the Corinthians who caused him so many headaches, "I always thank God for you because of his grace given you in Christ Jesus" (1 Corinthians 1:4). Let us not only ask God to meet the needs of these important people in our lives, but let us continually thank Him for the gifts that they are to our lives.

Pray the Scriptures:

John 17:6–19
Romans 1:8–10
Philippians 1:3–11

Focus Today:

In addition to a spouse, these friends can be close prayer partners for you. End a conversation with a close friend today by asking how you can pray for that person in the days ahead. And if the Spirit prompts you as you pray, write a note or pick up the phone and tell your friend so.

_____

_____

_____

_____

_____

_____

_____

_____

_____

_____

_____

_____

_____

_____

_____

_____

_____

_____

_____

_____

_____

_____

_____

I thank my God every time I remember you. (Philippians 1:3)

Week 2 Reflection

Five Myths About People Who Pray

When the subject of prayer comes up, most of us have a preconceived notion of what it means to be a person of prayer. But I wonder how many of these are true. Take a few minutes and reflect on why these myths aren't true of a person who is known for praying.

- You need to be an emotional person.

- You need to have a rather large religious vocabulary.

- You need to be a morning person, or at least not need much sleep.

- You need to feel like praying all the time.

- You need to be something other than completely normal.

Week 2 Reflection

_____

_____

_____

_____

_____

_____

_____

_____

_____

_____

_____

_____

_____

_____

_____

_____

_____

_____

_____

_____

_____

Week 3

Introduction

"Orange County is recession proof." That's what a handful of people told me as I interviewed to be a pastor there in 1988.

Fast forward a few years, and I was a pastor in Orange Country when the recession hit. The bottom fell out of the real estate market, and many people lost money. Our church attendance increased fifteen percent while our giving dropped ten percent. We had to stretch to minister to more people on less money.

We were behind $100,000 in our general fund budget when the time came to look at the next year's budget. We cut $200,000: the $100,000 to make up the shortfall and an additional $100,000 in case things didn't improve. We didn't want to fall behind in our payments. It was painful. I spent hours pouring over the budget, going line by line and cutting to the bone without knocking a wheel off the ministry.

Thanksgiving morning I was in my home office on my knees praying, and God impressed Psalm 126:4 on my heart: "Restore our fortunes, Lord, like streams in the Negev." I felt directed to begin to pray this verse. With this verse He promised the restoration of all that had been lost. For many months I focused on that verse, and I prayed, "God, You promised me You would do this. I just want to pray Your promise into being." It was not easy.

But one unsuspecting August Sunday morning, almost one year later, the offering was twice as large. A couple put a check in the offering that was equal to what a normal offering would be. They did not know that. They had just received an inheritance and felt they needed to tithe on it. Their obedience broke a dam. From that moment God started pouring provision into the church.

I prayed that verse and promise for months, but God has His timing and He answered.

Ready for Week 3?

During Week 3, the prayer journey moves to our communities of faith—our churches. We will pray for the corporate body as well as specific parts of the body. Take time this week to pray for needs of your church and pastors, ministry partners, and friends in your community.

_____

_____

_____

_____

_____

_____

_____

_____

_____

_____

_____

_____

_____

_____

_____

_____

_____

_____

_____

_____

_____

Day 1
Church Body

Ask Forgiveness

Paul spoke of "faith working through love" (Galatians 5:6), or in other words, our love towards others demonstrates our faith. Then in Ephesians 4:3, Paul calls us to "make every effort to keep the unity of the Spirit through the bond of peace." The life of the Spirit and unity with one another go together—and both are miracles.

Unfortunately, the enemy works to divide us, making that "every effort" Paul speaks of so necessary to maintaining our unity. It is easy to get hurt in church. We tend to have high expectations for one another, and we work closely enough together that we can get on each other's nerves. Or we end up fighting over personal preferences rather than the Christ-centered essentials of the church. Bitterness and unforgiveness set in, and the enemy scores a victory.

Jesus said in Mark 11:25 that when we stand in the place of prayer, we first need to forgive one another. Few things are more toxic to our spiritual lives and our prayer lives than unforgiveness. Jesus finished Mark 11:25 with "so that your Father in heaven may forgive you your sins." Our very relationship with God is at stake here.

Forgiving also frees us. In the words of William Klassen, "Forgiveness denies the destructive elements of our past from having power over our present." Forgiving people is not necessarily trusting them or minimizing the wrong done, but it is letting go and moving on, free to live and free to seek God.

Pray the Scriptures:

Micah 7:18–20
Matthew 6:9–15
Mark 11:24, 25

Focus Today:

Search your heart and ask God to reveal any unforgiveness you hold toward another. Confess that unforgiveness and walk away from it. If you need to make amends with someone, do so quickly.

_____

_____

_____

_____

_____

_____

_____

_____

_____

_____

_____

_____

_____

_____

_____

Who is a God like you, who pardons sin and forgives the transgression of the remnant of his inheritance? (Micah 7:18)

Day 2
Pastors and Staff

Buoy Your Pastor

> Have confidence in your leaders and submit to their authority, because they keep watch over you as those who must give an account. Do this so that their work will be a joy, not a burden, for that would be of no benefit to you. (Hebrews 13:17)

More than likely, this is a verse your pastor may feel awkward preaching. Yet that does not minimize its truth. One way to submit to your pastor's leadership and make it a joy for him or her is to pray for your pastor. There were many times when as a pastor I felt "buoyed up" with a power and composure for which I could not account. I would consciously feel that people were praying for me, and it made a tangible difference.

A pastor's job is quite complex. He or she wears at least five hats at a time—pastoral care-giver, preacher/teacher, business manager, organizational leader, and problem solver. Your pastor probably does not get paid what the corporate world pays for that level of leadership skill, but your prayers can make the difference!

Prayer is like a protective shield around your pastor and his or her family. When a church begins to move forward and reach outside its walls, the pastors and their families take the brunt of the spiritual warfare that comes against the church. In two of the great churches I pastored, an average of a hundred men volunteered to be my personal prayer partners. They picked a day of the week to pray specifically for me, and they prayed in teams once a month each through one of the Sunday morning services. Every day of the week and every Sunday morning when I preached, I was covered in prayer.

It is easy to complain about what your pastor does or does not do. Put yourself in a different place today and spend your time and words praying for your pastor. This is your chance to buoy him or her up and add joy to the work.

Pray the Scriptures:

Ephesians 6:19, 20
Hebrews 13:7, 17

Focus Today:

Pray for clarity of mind as your pastor balances the many priorities of the church. Ask God to protect your pastor and his or her family from spiritual attacks. Join others in the church as prayer partners for your pastoral staff.

_____

_____

_____

_____

_____

_____

_____

_____

_____

_____

Remember your leaders, who spoke the word of God to you. (Hebrews 13:7)

Day 3
Small Groups and Friends

Intercede for Others

In Ephesians, after listing the pieces of spiritual armor that every follower of Christ needs, Paul describes the one constant activity of the church, tying all of these elements of spiritual warfare together— "always keep on praying for all the saints" (Ephesians 6:18).

Here Paul specifically calls us to intercessory prayer. Intercession takes up faith-filled prayer on behalf of others; it calls out to God for them as you stand in their place. It is remarkable that God would respond to this kind of "proxy" praying, yet He does. Intercession paves the way for God's intervention in other people's lives and circumstances.

As you grow in intercessory prayer:

- Focus on the Spirit's help. A friend of mine once described his journey into intercession this way: "I used to start praying by first looking inside myself for the desire and strength to pray. It only pulled me down. But I decided to start my times of prayer by looking upward instead of inward, asking the Holy Spirit to come and teach me to pray. It changed everything."

- Keep prayer God-centered rather than problem-centered. Starting your prayer with praise is so important. Great intercessors often spend more time adoring God than asking Him for things. Prayer needs to be more than an exercise in worry.

- Stand on the merits of Christ's blood alone. Often at the heart of our spiritual insecurity is self-condemnation, afflicting us with a debilitating sense of unworthiness. I have frequently had to assert by faith, in spite of my feelings, that my standing before God is based solely on Christ's shed blood, not my impressiveness or self-righteousness.

Pray the Scriptures:

Ephesians 6:10–20
1 Timothy 2:1–4
James 5:13–18

Focus Today:

Who can you pray for in your church? Perhaps you know someone in a Sunday school class, a weekly small group, or just a close-knit group of friends who needs God to intervene. Pick two or three friends in the church and begin to intercede on behalf of that person.

_____

_____

_____

_____

_____

_____

_____

_____

_____

_____

*And pray in the Spirit on all occasions with all kinds of prayers and requests.
With this in mind, be alert and always keep on praying
for all the Lord's people. (Ephesians 6:18)*

Day 4
Youth and Young Adults

Think Young

Paul once wrote to the rather young man Timothy: "Don't let anyone look down on you because you are young" (1 Timothy 4:12). We must never underestimate the spiritual potential of the young people in our lives and in our churches.

Like many young people today, Timothy had some strikes against him. He had a complicated family background (Acts 16:1), he struggled with personal health issues (1 Timothy 5:23), he lived with high stress levels in his life (1:3, 4), and he tended to lack confidence (2 Timothy 1:6, 7).

Yet Paul assured Timothy that God did not give him a spirit of timidity but a spirit of power, love, and self-discipline (2 Timothy 1:7). Power is God's great energizer, love is God's great motivator, and self-discipline is God's great stabilizer. What a wonderful way to pray for the young people in our lives and churches!

By faith can you see a generation of young people the Lord would want to put His Spirit upon? Pray that He will raise up a consecrated generation that is energized with His power, motivated by His love, and stabilized with self-discipline in a self-indulgent world. Such a Spirit-anointed generation of young believers could change the world.

Pray the Scriptures:
2 Chronicles 34:1–5
Psalm 1:1–3
2 Timothy 1:6–8

Focus Today:
Pray for two or three young people in your life or in your church. Ask for God's power, love, and self-discipline to take over those young

people's hearts, minds, and spirits. Pray also for the Lord to raise up godly parents, mentors, and teachers for our young people.

_____

_____

_____

_____

_____

_____

_____

_____

_____

_____

_____

_____

_____

_____

_____

_____

For this reason I remind you to fan into flame the gift of God,
which is in you through the laying on of my hands. (2 Timothy 1:6)

Day 5
Children

Love the Children

May the words of Jesus in Mark 10:14 never lose their clarity in setting the priorities of our church life: "Let the little children come to me." The disciples, in their all too adult world, were pushing the children aside and missing God's heart. Jesus loves the children, and they are to be our inspiration. He says that we need the simple faith of a child to see the kingdom of Heaven, so let us pray for their hearts to remain pure and their faith uncomplicated.

From God's perspective the most vulnerable among us are our greatest responsibility. Today a war is being waged in modern society against children—from abortion to broken families to child abuse to human trafficking to the moral pollution of their hearts and minds at very young ages. We need to pray for their protection and welfare.

Nearly half of all Americans who accept Jesus as Savior do so before age thirteen. I gave my heart fully to Christ as an eight-year-old child, and I will never forget the fire of God's Spirit in my young heart. Pray that the children in our churches will have a similar living encounter with Jesus Christ at an early age and that the fire of the Holy Spirit will take root in their souls.

Pray the Scriptures:
Exodus 22:22, 23
Mark 10:13–16

Focus Today:
Pray for the salvation of our children, for godly teachers and role models in their lives, and for the fire of the Holy Spirit in their hearts.

_____

_____

_____

_____

_____

_____

_____

_____

_____

_____

_____

_____

_____

_____

_____

_____

_____

_____

_____

_____

_____

_____

_____

"Let the little children come to me, and do not hinder them,
for the kingdom of God belongs to such as these." (Mark 10:14)

Day 6
Local Outreach

Reach the Locals

When I was a new pastor at Central Assembly in Springfield, Missouri, a young housewife in her thirties had a vision to teach handbells to students at the middle school next door. I had never put junior high students and church handbells together before, but she wanted to do something to make a connection with people outside the walls of our church.

When the Christmas season came around, she asked if her students could play a Christmas carol in a Sunday morning service. As they played in their less-than-professional way, I sensed something beginning to happen in the crowd. When they finished, two thousand people stood to their feet, cheering and applauding. As the ovation went on and on, I sensed a release in the spirit of the church—I saw the face of Jesus as He began to smile. From that time forward, outreach ministry through the church seemed effortless as God spoke creatively to people and the congregation mobilized to reach outside itself.

Jesus said that the harvest is plentiful but the laborers are few. Then He called us, not to pray for the harvest, but to pray for laborers and workers in His harvest (Matthew 9:37, 38). God's plan is not just programs, but people who carry His heart and do something about it. Local outreach events are needed, but without laborers called to God's harvest, they are just more activity.

Pray the Scriptures:
Proverbs 31:8, 9
Isaiah 61:1–3
Matthew 25:35, 36

Focus Today:

Pray for volunteers in your church and join with two or three others to pray and think creatively about ways to touch the lives of people outside the church. Pray for tangible opportunities to meet their practical needs but also to verbalize the gospel of Jesus Christ.

_____

_____

_____

_____

_____

_____

_____

_____

_____

_____

_____

_____

_____

_____

_____

For I was hungry and you gave me something to eat,
I was thirsty and you gave me something to drink,
I was a stranger and you invited me in. (Matthew 25:35)

Day 7
Discipleship

The Need to Disciple

The goal of discipleship is found in 2 Timothy 3:17—that every believer "be thoroughly equipped for every good work." And the means to that end is found in the previous verse: "All Scripture is God-breathed and is useful for teaching, rebuking, correcting and training in righteousness" (verse 16). The Word of God is our template for discipleship; its proclamation and application are the process:

- Teaching – what we need to believe

- Rebuking – what we need to stop doing

- Correcting – what we need to start doing

- Training – what we need to become

Let's ask who the gifted teachers and preachers in our churches are. Who will help implement the Word so that discipleship happens in our lives? We need to pray for those teachers and preachers, honor them and thank God for them, and we need to pray that the Lord will raise up more people to teach and disciple other believers.

In addition to being taught by others, we must also read, study, and pray God's Word personally, learning to feed ourselves. When we learn to feed ourselves spiritually, we cross a wonderful line of spiritual maturity and open ourselves up to a lifestyle of listening to the Lord and following Him more fully. This moves us beyond inspirational Sunday morning services. This brings us to intentional investment in the accountable growth of other believers.

Pray the Scriptures:

John 15:1–17
Acts 2:42–47
2 Timothy 3:10–17

Focus Today:

Pray for increased understanding of God's Word in your personal study as well as in the study of the teachers and preachers in your church. Ask God for discipleship partners.

_____

_____

_____

_____

_____

_____

_____

_____

_____

_____

_____

_____

_____

_____

_____

_____

I am the vine; you are the branches. If you remain in me and I in you, you will bear much fruit; apart from me you can do nothing. (John 15:5)

Week 3 Reflection
Desperation Praying

How many times have I not known what to do, not known where to turn, or not known what the human solution would be. This is where desperation praying enters. It is desperation kind of prayer that says, "God, without You, there will be no breakthrough."

Jehoshaphat came under attack by an alliance of three nations. He knew that the situation in the natural realm was hopeless. He called the people of Jerusalem and Judah to pray and fast. In 2 Chronicles 20:6–12, we have his recorded prayer. Let's look at the first and last verses of his prayer.

Great praying begins with praise, where we do not focus on the problem but on God and His attributes that are bigger than the problem. This is exactly how Jehoshaphat prayed: "LORD, the God of our ancestors, are you not the God who is in heaven? You rule over all the kingdoms of the nations. Power and might are in your hand, and no one can withstand you." He focused on three things: God's supremacy, authority, and capacity. What a way to begin praying!

He then closed the prayer: "For we have no power to face this vast army that is attacking us. We do not know what to do, but our eyes are on you." This is desperation praying. It is not a lack of faith to not know what to do. Rather it is self-sufficiency to tell God that you have it figured out. Jehoshaphat ended his prayer, and God sent a prophet: "Do not be afraid or discouraged because of this vast army. For the battle is not yours, but God's." God will do that for us. He will take the battle into His own hands, since we belong to Him. Our enemies become His enemies.

God loves us to live in desperation. It is often the edge of faith. And it is when we say, "We do not know what to do, but our eyes are on you," that He takes over the battle for us.

Week 3 Reflection

_____

_____

_____

_____

_____

_____

_____

_____

_____

_____

_____

_____

_____

_____

_____

_____

_____

_____

_____

Week 4

Introduction

I was a freshman at Winona State University when I met Duane. This guy loved God ferociously. He practiced what I call "discipleship by dragging around." He discipled me by taking me to prayer meetings, campus ministry meetings, and leadership meetings.

Duane was good at picking locks. During my sophomore year, we picked the lock of an old stone church on the edge of campus and spent three afternoons every week praying for the campus. In those prayer times, my friend taught me how to intercede. He laid on his face on the church platform and cried out to God. It shook my world. Sometimes I would just sit and watch him because I had never seen someone my age act like that. Little did I know what I would walk through two years later at the University of Minnesota.

A girl I knew on campus and I argued about baptism of the Spirit. Near the end of that school year she was baptized in the Spirit in her dorm room. God filled her, and then unleashed a river of His Spirit on the campus. I have never seen anything like it in a secular setting. Students were saved and filled in the Spirit all over campus. God sent an awakening to Winona State.

I left for the University of Minnesota, and under my leadership, the Chi Alpha group there shrank down to nothing. I found myself spread out on the floor of the campus ministry office praying like Duane. God moved on the campus, which led me to be the full-time pastor of the university church. There was an intern from North Central University with us who felt led to start a Chi Alpha group at Winona State. After a couple tough years getting started, that group experienced a breakthrough. Eventually it needed the largest auditorium on campus for the weekly service, but it wasn't available every week. So they bought this old stone church on the edge of campus—the same one where Duane and I had picked the lock and prayed.

It has been over forty years since I was at Winona State, and I return every year to help students who are involved in a thriving Chi Alpha ministry prepare for their ministry credentials. Last year a Chinese student came up to me and said, "I came to Winona State from China not knowing anything about Jesus. God saved me. I am the answer to your prayer." I do believe that God answers prayers long into the future. Even now, He takes the prayers invested in that campus and says, "I'm going to answer these prayers for many, many years to come."

Ready for Week 4?

In our final week of this prayer journey, our focus moves beyond our homes and community to our nation and the world. This week pray for a spiritual awakening in the churches of America to reach both our country and the world with the message of Christ.

_____

_____

_____

_____

_____

_____

_____

_____

_____

_____

_____

_____

_____

_____

_____

_____

_____

_____

_____

Day 1
The President & Washington DC

Pray for Our National Leaders

God clearly mandates followers of Jesus to pray for those holding positions of civic authority (1 Timothy 2:1, 2). We influence the direction and welfare of our nation this way. In fact, Paul seems to infer a direct link between praying for kings and the ability to live peaceful and quiet lives.

Today's call to pray for national leaders must rise above personal politics. Paul called the church to pray for the Roman emperors and their underlings—political leaders who were in large part brutal, power-hungry, and perverted. These officials were not the kind of people we would want voted into office, and yet Paul puts them at the top of our prayer lists. As a pastor I have heard people say, "I just can't bring myself to pray for our president because I so resent everything he stands for." Yet as citizens of a kingdom not of this world, we must be bigger than that. This has nothing to do with politics and everything to do with God's capacity to direct and guide our leaders, no matter who they are.

As God's people, we also need to keep our attitudes in check. The political rhetoric these days is so harsh and adversarial that it can infect our own spirits in ungodly ways. But Paul in Romans 13 reminds us that secular governing authorities are part of God's plan for us, and so we are to give them what we owe them: "if respect, then respect; if honor, then honor" (Romans 13:7).

Pray the Scriptures:

Romans 13:1–7
1 Timothy 2:1–7
1 Peter 2:13–17

Focus Today:

Pray for our president, vice president, and those who work closely with them. Pray for our country's senators and representatives in the US Congress. Pray for the nine Supreme Court justices. Ask the Holy Spirit to rest upon Washington DC and the churches that serve the city.

_____

_____

_____

_____

_____

_____

_____

_____

_____

_____

_____

_____

_____

_____

Let everyone be subject to the governing authorities, for there is no authority except that which God has established. (Romans 13:1)

Day 2
Local Leaders

Pray for Your Local Leaders

I served as a pastor in Springfield, Missouri, for several years and during that time another local pastor in a leading Springfield church took the initiative to host a luncheon for other pastors (like me) every few months.

This was more than just lunch, though. The pastor invited one city leader to each lunch and interviewed them for fifteen minutes after the meal. The interview gave us opportunity to understand the pressures and challenges these leaders faced in the community and to ask them how we could pray for them. Local leaders who attended included the mayor, police and fire chiefs, the school district superintendent, and the chair of the county board of supervisors. Some were Christians, others not; some were Democrats, others Republican and Independents. But no matter who they were, they could all answer the question: How can we pray for you?

Each luncheon lasted only one hour, but we left much more in touch with our local leaders and their needs. Even those we disagreed with politically were "humanized" as we heard them describe needs in their families, stresses on their jobs, and ways they felt the church could serve the community.

The influence of these local leaders sometimes touches us more personally than leaders in federal government. These leaders protect our cities, educate our children, plan our communities, repair our roads, and run our utilities. In Springfield I was also able to gain the favor and endorsement of both the mayor and school district superintendent through the local compassion ministries of the church where I served.

We have the privilege as Christ's living church both to pray for and to serve our local leaders—to be salt and light in our local worlds.

Pray the Scriptures:

Psalm 55:22
Philippians 2:1–4
2 Corinthians 1:3, 4

Focus Today:

Allow the Holy Spirit to lead you as you pray for local leaders today. Pray for people God lays on your heart specifically. Lift up their families, their health, and the decisions they face on a daily basis.

_____

_____

_____

_____

_____

_____

_____

_____

_____

_____

_____

. . . so that we can comfort those in any trouble with the comfort
we ourselves receive from God. (2 Corinthians 1:4)

Day 3
Spiritual Awakening in Our Country

Pray for Spiritual Awakening

Our country is in need of a spiritual awakening. We draw our direction for today's prayer from 2 Chronicles 7:14.

> "If my people . . . humble themselves"

Repent of spiritual coldness, indifference, prayerlessness, and disobedience in our lives and churches. Seek God for authentic humility and dependence on Him to mark our way forward.

> "If my people . . . pray and seek my face"

Hunger for God to pour out His Spirit in our churches with miraculous power and evangelistic effectiveness. Ask God to do whatever it takes to turn people back to God and encounter Jesus in our nation.

> "If my people . . . turn from their wicked ways"

Repent of unholy affections and ungodly behavior in our personal lives and our churches. Seek God to turn back the sins of immorality, pornography, abortion, materialism, prejudice, and injustice in our nation.

Praise God now for His response:

> "Then will I hear from heaven and will forgive their sin and will heal their land."

Pray the Scriptures:
Psalm 85
Ezekiel 37:1–14
Matthew 5:13–16
Ephesians 5:8–20

Focus Today:

Pray specifically for the churches of America to repent and seek after God. Praise God for the mercy and grace that He will shower on us as we humble ourselves before Him.

_____

_____

_____

_____

_____

_____

_____

_____

_____

_____

_____

_____

_____

_____

_____

_____

*You are the salt of the earth. But if the salt loses its saltiness,
how can it be made salty again? (Matthew 5:13)*

Day 4
The Persecuted Church

Pray for the Persecuted Church

Conflicts around the world are our present day reality. Jesus said that wars and rumors of wars would mark the end times. We cannot pray them away, so how do we pray? We pray for wisdom for national leaders and for the effectiveness of international diplomacy. We pray for Christ's living church in nations in conflict, that it will be strong and that believers, in spite of suffering, will walk through the open doors that war creates to minister to others and share the hope of the gospel.

Beyond the conflicts between nations or within nations, there is an even more pervasive worldwide conflict—the war against followers of Christ in the persecuted church. There has been more persecution in the twentieth century than the previous nineteen centuries combined, and most of it against Christians. Every day believers are being arrested, raped, tortured, and killed for the simple reason that they will not renounce Christ.

These are our brothers and sisters in the Lord. I personally know a college professor with a PhD in mathematics who has languished in prison in a foreign country for years because of his Christian faith and influence. My friend has also been leading people to Christ in prison.

This reminds us to pray that the persecuted church will suffer in a way that honors the Lord, experience the supernatural, sustaining presence of the Holy Spirit, and carry a bold witness for the gospel of Jesus Christ without bitterness or hatred toward its tormentors.

Pray the Scriptures:

Philippians 1:12–14
Colossians 4:2–4
2 Corinthians 12:9, 10
Hebrews 13:3

Focus Today:

As you pray for the Christians of the persecuted church today, use the Lord's Prayer as a model. Pray that their daily provisions will be met, that they will forgive their persecutors, that they will not fall into temptation, and that they will experience supernatural intervention.

And because of my chains, most of the brothers and sisters have become confident in the Lord and dare all the more to proclaim the gospel without fear. (Philippians 1:14)

Day 5
Missionaries

Pray for Our Missionaries

I have but one candle of life to burn,
and would rather burn it out where people are dying in darkness
than in a land which is flooded with light.
—Unknown

Missionaries answer God's call and leave home and family to reach
a people for whom God has burdened them. When we refer to
missionaries, we likely think first of those who have moved to far-off
places or those who must to live undercover in a country closed to the
gospel. They have counted the cost and will risk their lives for Christ.

But let's not forget the missionaries working in the United States
among our own unreached or hard-to-reach. Even though America is
a free country, sharing the gospel can be just as difficult as our society
becomes increasingly less Christian. These missionaries also counted
the cost and joyfully accepted the mission before them—church
planting among Muslims, reaching students on university campuses,
serving youth and adults with drug and alcohol problems, or providing
care to our soldiers.

All of these missionaries, both near and far, need encouragement and
prayer as they work in difficult places and in difficult situations. A lost
soul is a lost soul, no matter what country that person lives in or what
tribe they come from. The enemy will do what it takes to keep them
that way. Pray for our missionaries, that as they encounter discourag-
ing moments or seasons, or outright spiritual warfare, they will stand
firm on God's Great Commission to go and His great promise that all
nations, tribes, and tongues will gather at His throne.

Pray the Scriptures:

Romans 10:9–17
Colossians 4:2–4

Focus Today:

Pray for the missionaries who minister in the United States and the military chaplains currently serving around the world and in the United States. Ask God to meet their spiritual, physical, and financial needs.

_____

_____

_____

_____

_____

_____

_____

_____

_____

_____

_____

_____

And how can they hear without someone preaching to them? And how can anyone preach unless they are sent? (Romans 10:14)

Day 6
Unreached Peoples

Pray for Unreached People

Oswald J. Smith said, "No one has the right to hear the gospel twice, while there remains someone who has not heard it once." On the island of Pemba off the coast of Tanzania between the mainland and Zanzibar, 300,000 people call this island home. Completely Islamic, there is only a 0.01 percent possibility that these folks will ever hear the gospel of Jesus Christ—once.

According to the Joshua Project, there are 7,081 unreached people groups with a population of 2.9 billion people. With a world population nearing seven billion, this means 41.7 percent of the world's population is yet unreached; they have less than 2 percent evangelical followers of Jesus among them.

The Somali are the largest people group on the Horn of Africa. They number just over sixteen million people in Somalia, Ethiopia, Kenya, and Djibouti. Like the people on Pemba, less than 0.01 percent of Somali people are followers of Jesus, and only 6 percent of non-Christians in Somaliland know a Christian.

Who will reach these people? Who will take the gospel to the places that it has yet to be heard? Jesus commanded His disciples to pray for laborers for the harvest. Though you may not be called to live among an unreached people, you are called to pray. Pray for the missionaries God has called and will call, not only from America but also from other countries.

Pray the Scriptures:

Matthew 24:14
Revelation 5:9, 10
Revelation 7:9, 10

Focus Today:

Pray that the hearts of 2.9 billion people would be stirred towards the gospel. Pray that laborers would answer God's call to reach His harvest on Pemba, and pray for the safety of workers in Somalia and those serving among Somali people in neighboring countries.

_____

_____

_____

_____

_____

_____

_____

_____

_____

_____

_____

_____

_____

_____

_____

After this I looked, and there before me was a great multitude that no one
could count, from every nation, tribe, people and language,
standing before the throne of the Lamb. (Revelation 7:9)

Day 7
A Mobilized Church

Pray for a Mobilized Church

There will never be enough missionaries to reach the 2.9 billion unreached people who have yet to hear the gospel. The whole church everywhere must mobilize to reach them. That does not mean you need a passport, a new set of luggage, and a call to the Dark Canyon of the Euphrates, because God is moving people to the places He needs them. He is bringing unreached peoples to the parts of the world where the church is already established. There are more people on the move around the world today than at any other point in history. One in every thirty-five persons now lives in a country other than where he or she was born.*

The migration of peoples is happening and there are two ways to view it—with fear or with hope. Let's take the example of Islam. You can be afraid that Islam is marching westward and is intent on overtaking Christianity, or you can believe that God is moving Muslims to the West so they can hear the gospel in a free country. Which will you choose—a spirit of fear toward a false religion or a spirit of power in the certain hope of Christ?

Migration is one of today's defining global issues, and we in the church must be ready to engage the people moving our way. In today's global world we are all missionaries of some kind. Are we ready to love and build relationships with the immigrants and refugees who are making America their new home? Is our heart one with Christ's to see that the lost are found? Or are we holding the unfamiliar at arm's length? Let's embrace the hope of Christ and the power of Spirit to see the unreached reached.

*Patrick Johnstone, *The Future of the Global Church* (Downers Grive, Ill.: InterVarsity Press, 2012).

Pray the Scriptures:
Zechariah 8:20–22
Matthew 28:16–20
John 12:23–26

Focus Today:
Relinquish any fear or stereotypes you hold for unfamiliar or unknown cultures and religions. Ask God to bring a new friend or neighbor from another culture or religion into your life, and fully embrace the hope of the gospel and the power of the Holy Spirit to change hearts.

_____

_____

_____

_____

_____

_____

_____

_____

_____

_____

_____

And many peoples and powerful nations will come to Jerusalem to seek the LORD Almighty and to entreat him. (Zechariah 8:22)

Week 4 Reflection

Ten Keys for a Growing Prayer Life

As you conclude Week 4 of this prayer journey, know that this journey is only beginning. As you move forward on the path God is laying before you, keep these ten keys in mind:

1. Keep prayer God-centered rather than problem-centered.

2. See prayer as a privilege rather than a duty.

3. Let faith be Christ-centered rather than technique-centered.

4. Focus on the Spirit's help rather than your skill.

5. Enter by Christ's blood rather than your merits.

6. Embrace Christ's authority rather than Satan's lies.

7. Exercise prayer like a victor rather than a victim.

8. Build prayer around God's Word rather than your will.

9. Pray regularly rather than occasionally.

10. Approach prayer as an encounter rather than a request.

Week 4 Reflection

_____

_____

_____

_____

_____

_____

_____

_____

_____

_____

_____

_____

_____

_____

_____

_____

_____

_____

_____

_____

_____

About the Author

Dr. James T. Bradford holds a PhD in Aerospace Engineering from the University of Minnesota. As a student he led a small Chi Alpha campus Bible study that eventually grew into a university church. Upon graduation in 1979, Bradford stepped into full time ministry with that campus outreach. In 1988, Bradford and his family moved to Southern California where he pastored Newport-Mesa Christian Center in the heart of Orange County. Twelve years later the Bradfords transitioned to Vancouver, BC, to pastor  Broadway Church, a move that returned Jim to his early Canadian roots. It was in 2003 that Bradford and his family moved to Springfield to assume the pastorate of Central Assembly.

In 2009, Dr. Bradford was elected General Secretary of the Assemblies of God, and serves as a member of the Executive Leadership Team and the Executive Presbytery for the Assemblies of God. As general secretary, Bradford oversees Ministerial Resourcing, the credentialing of ministers, church chartering, the collection of official statistics, and the Flower Pentecostal Heritage Center.

He is author of *Preaching: Maybe It Is Rocket Science*.

Jim Bradford and his wife, Sandi, have two daughters.

How to Order More Copies

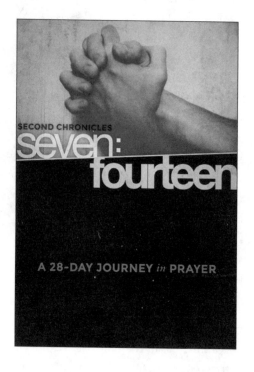

To order more copies of this book visit

www.myhealthychurch.com